Unmasking Halloween

A Comprehensive Study of History and Traditions

By

Ewan Pratt

Contents

Introduction

Once upon a time, in a small, picturesque town nestled between rolling hills and a tranquil river, there lived a young girl named Lily. Lily had always been intrigued by the enigmatic charm of Halloween. As the leaves began to change and the air turned crisp, her excitement grew with each passing day. Halloween, for her, was not just a holiday; it was an enchanting journey into the realms of the unknown.

Lily's fascination with Halloween was something she had inherited from her grandmother, Agnes, a woman with a wealth of knowledge about the holiday's history and traditions. Agnes had told Lily stories about the ancient Celtic festival of Samhain, when the boundary between the living and the dead blurred, and people lit bonfires to ward off malevolent spirits. She had shared tales of the mysterious origins of jack-o'-lanterns, carved to scare away wandering souls.

Each year, as October painted the town in shades of orange and black, Lily and her grandmother would embark on a quest to prepare for Halloween.
They would spend hours crafting intricate costumes, with Agnes sewing and Lily adding imaginative touches. Their house transformed into a sanctuary of cobwebs, pumpkins, and eerie decor. Together, they would explore the town's history and local legends, seeking out the best spots for trick-or-treating and hidden treasures of folklore.

As Halloween approached, Lily's fascination with the holiday only deepened. She could feel the ancient magic that seemed to linger in the autumn air, and she eagerly anticipated the Halloween night, when the veil between the worlds was thinnest. On that special night, she believed anything was possible.

One crisp October evening, as Lily and her grandmother prepared to set out for their annual adventure, Agnes shared a secret. She led Lily to a hidden nook in the attic, unveiling an antique book filled with spells and incantations related to Halloween. "This book has been passed down through our family for generations," Agnes whispered. "On Halloween night, it has the power to grant one wish." But remember, Lily, wishes come with great responsibility."

Overwhelmed by the magnitude of the gift, Lily pondered her wish carefully. She wanted to share the enchantment of Halloween with everyone in her town. So, on Halloween night, with the full moon illuminating her path, Lily cast her wish. In an instant, her town transformed into a fantastical realm of ghouls, wizards, and fairy-tale creatures. The river sparkled with magical lights, and laughter filled the air.

Lily's wish had come true, but she realized that the responsibility was to ensure the magic lived on. The next year, she began teaching other children about the history and traditions of Halloween, just as her grandmother had taught her. The town's fascination with Halloween grew, and it became a place where people from near and far gathered to celebrate the enchanting holiday.

Through Lily's efforts, Halloween evolved into a holiday that bridged generations, honoring its history while embracing the creativity and wonder of the present. The fascination with Halloween, ignited by a young girl's curiosity and her grandmother's wisdom, had turned a small town into a place where magic and history intertwined, making Halloween a cherished celebration for all.

In this book, we shall embark on a trip similar to Lily's in her little village. Our goal is to dive into the history and traditions that have helped to make Halloween such an enduring and valued part of our worldwide cultural fabric. We will look at the holiday's ancient beginnings, its evolution over ages, and its expansion to every corner of the globe.

We hope to reveal the intriguing narrative of a festival that has the potential to fascinate and mystify, just as Lily found the power of Halloween to bring her village to life with enchantment and wonder. This book takes us beyond a cursory awareness of Halloween, offering insight on its history, traditions, disputes, and cultural relevance.

As we proceed through the pages that follow, you will discover not only the rich history of Halloween, but also the numerous ways it has been celebrated and altered. We'll follow the threads of the holiday's past and present, looking at the influence of literature, film, and pop culture, as well as its impact on social movements and communities throughout the world.

Halloween, as we know it today, is not merely a day for children to collect candies or adults to indulge in costume parties. It is a celebration that connects us to our past, resonates with our present, and casts its shadow into our future. Our goal is to unmask the mysteries of Halloween, inviting you to join us on this spellbinding journey.

Chapter 1
Ancient Origins

Halloween has rich and complicated roots that may be traced back to ancient customs. At its heart, Halloween derives from the ancient Celtic holiday of Samhain, which marked the end of the harvest season and the onset of winter. The origins of Halloween are a fascinating trip through ancient peoples' rituals and beliefs.

1. Samhain is the Celtic New Year.

Samhain, pronounced "sow-in," was a significant date in the Celtic calendar. It was celebrated around October 31st and marked the conclusion of the harvest and the start of the darker half of the year. This transition was a moment when the barrier between the living and the dead was at its thinnest for the Celts. During Samhain, they thought that the ghosts of the dead returned to the mortal realm.

Lighting of Bonfires: was one of the most important rituals of Samhain. These flames were thought to have protective and purifying characteristics, aiding in the warding off of evil spirits. The Celts would frequently construct big community bonfires and congregate around them to offer sacrifices and perform divination.

Costumes: To hide from the spirits who roamed the land, the Celts wore costumes made of animal skins and heads, and they frequently engaged in ceremonial dances and games. This practice of dressing up to pacify or fend off ghosts has continued and evolved into the present Halloween costume celebration.

2. Roman Influence

Feralia and **Pomona**, two fall festivals celebrated by the ancient Romans, imprinted their impact on Halloween.

Feralia: Feralia was a late-October Roman festival dedicated to remembering the departed. To pacify the spirits of the dead, Romans would leave food and gifts, similar to the present practice of placing offerings at gravesites.

Pomona: The Romans also observed Pomona, a festival honoring the goddess of fruit and plants. Apples were extremely significant at Pomona, and the familiar Halloween pastime of bobbing for apples had its origins in this Roman festival.

3. Christianization of Samhain

As the Roman Empire extended and Christian influences increased, the Celtic festival of Samhain progressively changed. Religious observances were intended to replace pagan holidays by the Christian church. To coincide with Samhain, All Hallow's Eve (October 31st) and All Saints' Day (November 1st) were founded to celebrate and pray for the souls of Christian saints and the departed.

In this way, the Celtic holiday of Samhain was Christianized, including themes of remembrance for the deceased and saints' feasts. This combination of customs provided the groundwork for the Halloween we know today.

The ancient beginnings of Halloween in Samhain and its incorporation of Roman rituals constitute the initial layers of a celebration that has evolved over millennia. These old rituals are the ancestral ghosts that haunt and enchant our modern Halloween celebration. In the pages that follow, we will travel through time to discover how these traditions grew and intermingled with the rituals of numerous nations, resulting in the colorful and intriguing festival that we celebrate today.

Chapter 2

Halloween in the Middle Ages

As Halloween progressed through history, the medieval period saw substantial modifications to the celebration, eventually leading to the Halloween we know today. During this period, Halloween was a complex mixing of Christian and pagan themes, beliefs, and rituals that resulted in a distinct blend of remembrance for the dead and joyful merriment.

1. All Hallow's Eve and All Saints' Day

The Christian Church had a strong effect on medieval Halloween, as it had on its predecessors. All Hallow's Eve, celebrated on October 31st, was a predecessor to Halloween and a night dedicated to remembering the dead. The following day, November 1st, was All Saints' Day, a Christian holiday commemorating saints and martyrs. These two days were inextricably linked to medieval Halloween customs.

Church Bells: Throughout the night on All Hallow's Eve, the church bells would ring to signify the commencement of the solemn ceremony. These bell ringings were thought to aid the souls of the deceased on their journey to the afterlife.

2. Guising and Soul Cakes

Medieval Halloween was also a time for almsgiving and charity. In exchange for little, delicious pastries known as soul cakes, the impoverished would go door to door singing songs and offering to pray for the souls of the homeowners' departed relatives. This custom is seen as the forerunner of modern-day trick-or-treating.

Another medieval Halloween practice was guising, in which individuals, mainly children, dressed up in costumes and went from house to home, reading poetry or singing songs in return for food or money. Guising evolved into the present activity of trick-or-treating, in which youngsters dress up in costumes and collect candy.

3. The Invention of Jack-o'-Lanterns

The tradition of carving jack-o'-lanterns began to take shape during the medieval period. Turnips were originally hollowed out and fashioned with hideous faces to use as lights to fend off bad spirits. After Irish immigrants introduced the notion to the United States, this ritual grew into the pumpkin carving we associate with Halloween today.

Medieval Halloween was a complicated and varied event, with its combination of Christian veneration for the dead and the growing practice of guising and soul cakes. It marked a change from older, more somber and spiritual observances to the more cheerful, celebratory practices that would characterize Halloween in the contemporary day.

In the pages that follow, we will look at how Halloween evolved over the centuries, impacted by literature, culture, and the distinctive rituals of many locations. The medieval period established Halloween as a festival of transition, where the past met the present and the serious combined with the fun, resulting in a complex tapestry of traditions and practices that enchant and beguile us even now.

Chapter 3
The First American Halloween

Halloween began to take on a particular character in North America when European settlers carried their rituals to the New World. The early American Halloween was a mash-up of Old World rituals, Native American influences, and the growing nation's ingenuity. It marked the start of this treasured holiday's distinctly American celebration.

1. Colonial Influence

Early American Halloween festivities were heavily inspired by **English and Scottish settlers'** traditions. These European settlers brought practices like lighting bonfires, fortune-telling, and the practice of soul cakes with them. However, Halloween in America would quickly morph into something distinctively American.

Fortune-Telling: Fortune-telling was a popular activity during early American Halloween. On this night, young people believed they might foretell their future marriages. Apple peeling, mirror gazing, and nut-cracking divination were among the techniques used.

2. The Invention of Pumpkin Carving

The habit of carving jack-o'-lanterns began to take shape during the early American Halloween. However, turnips were initially utilized instead of pumpkins. To stave off evil spirits, the settlers carved turnips with creepy faces. This ritual would evolve in the nineteenth century, when Irish immigrants brought the pumpkin as the favored carving medium, which was more plentiful in the United States.

3. Utilizing Native American Traditions

Early American Halloween festivities incorporated certain elements of Native American rituals. During the harvest season, Native American tribes held their own feasts and ceremonies. As a result of this cultural interchange, early American Halloween celebrations included cornhusk dolls and corn mazes.

4. Harvest Festivals in Season

In the early days of Halloween in America, the event was intimately associated with harvest festivities. To celebrate the end of the agricultural season, communities would gather for feasts, games, and other activities. It was a time of thanksgiving for a great harvest as well as superstitions related with the arrival of winter.

Early American Halloween was a melting pot of rituals that reflected the diversity and ingenuity of the New World's people. It was a time when the holiday was still growing and responding to the country's particular climate and cultural influences.

In the following parts, we will look at how early American Halloween laid the ground for Halloween to become a distinctly American holiday. We'll go back to the Victorian era to see how Halloween became popular as a social and romantic festival, and how it eventually evolved into the contemporary holiday we know and love today.

Chapter 4

Halloween in the Victorian Era

The Victorian era, with its focus on etiquette, romance, and a love for the arts, was instrumental in turning Halloween into the celebration we know today. Halloween grew from a modest, rather rustic event to a more spectacular and socially significant affair throughout this time period. Victorian Halloween was a unique combination of custom, superstition, and rising consumerism.

1. Making the Holiday More Romantic

Halloween was no exception to the Victorians' tendency for romanticizing rituals. Halloween began to be observed as a celebration of love and courting during this time period. To forecast their future romantic partners, young people would play divination games. Love and marriage superstitions were widely spread.

Apple Peeling: Apple peeling was a popular divination game in which young ladies would peel an apple in one continuous strip, and the length of the peel was thought to indicate the initial of their future spouse.

Mirror-Gazing: Another popular divination exercise involves looking into a mirror at midnight in the hopes of seeing their future love's face mirrored in the glass.

2. Development of Party Games and Fortune Telling

A vast variety of party games and fortune-telling activities emerged during Victorian Halloween. These activities were frequently lively and flirty, reflecting the era's emphasis on courting.

Bobbing for Apples: A popular Victorian Halloween pastime, this old Roman practice was resurrected during the colonial period. In a tub of water, young people would try to capture apples with their teeth.

Snap-Apple: A game in which apples were strung together and participants sought to eat the apple without using their hands. It was not only entertaining, but it frequently resulted in hilarious and flirty conversations.

3. The Literature's Role

Halloween was frequently depicted in literature throughout the Victorian era, which was a time of tremendous creative success. Halloween sceneries were frequently featured in poems, short tales, and illustrated publications. Halloween motifs were interwoven into works by authors such as Edgar Allan Poe and Washington Irving, contributing to the holiday's mystery.

4. Halloween Parties

Halloween parties as we know them now emerged during the Victorian era. Similar to current Halloween parties, these gatherings featured spectacular décor, extravagant costumes, and a variety of games and diversions. The emphasis was not just on divination but also on community fun.

The Victorian Halloween saw a huge shift in the emphasis of the festival. It evolved into a day of socializing, courting, and creation. As time passed, Halloween evolved, inspired by literature, popular culture, and the commercialization that arose throughout this century.

In the next chapters, we will look at the modernization of Halloween, its commercialization, the impact of literature and film, and the birth of iconic Halloween rituals. Halloween's place in popular culture and as a treasured festival of creativity and magic was established during the Victorian era.

Chapter 5

Modern Halloween

The growth of Halloween into the modern celebration we know today is a story of cultural fusion, commercialization, and the persistent pull of tradition. From its ancient roots to the Victorian era, Halloween has experienced considerable modifications, and the move into the modern age brought about more developments that have made it a genuinely worldwide celebration.

1. Commercialization and Mass Production

The 20th century was a crucial turning point in the history of Halloween. The holiday underwent a boom in commercialization. The development of department shops and the advent of the greeting card business introduced Halloween-themed items to the people. Costumes, decorations, and novelty things became readily accessible.

Trick-or-Treating: One of the most enduring traditions of modern Halloween, trick-or-treating, gained popularity during this time. Children would dress up in costumes and go door-to-door collecting candy from their neighbors. It became a community and family-friendly pastime.

2. The Influence of Pop Culture

Hollywood and popular culture played a big part in defining modern Halloween. Horror films, television programs, and literature added to the holiday's focus on ghosts, monsters, and all things scary. Iconic creatures like Dracula, Frankenstein's monster, and witches became mainstays of Halloween costumes.

Disney's Influence: Walt Disney's launch of Mickey's Not-So-Scary Halloween Party at Disneyland in the 1950s brought Halloween to an even broader audience. Disney's family-friendly approach helped to make Halloween a treasured holiday for children and parents alike.

3. The Rise of Halloween Parties

Halloween celebrations grew from its Victorian beginnings into grandiose gatherings in the modern period. These gatherings featured lavish décor, innovative costumes, and a wide selection of games, making Halloween a pleasant occasion for all ages. Many adults also embraced Halloween as a time for humorous and inventive self-expression.

4. The Influence of Television

Television had a crucial part in the popularization of Halloween. Classic TV specials, including "It's the Great Pumpkin, Charlie Brown" and "The Legend of Sleepy Hollow", were fixtures of the Christmas season. In recent years, Halloween-themed episodes of famous programs have helped keep the spirit of the occasion alive.

5. The Impact on Retail

Modern Halloween has become a multibillion-dollar industry. Seasonal boutiques, dedicated completely to Halloween, develop each year, selling everything from costumes and decorations to candy and haunted house attractions. The holiday has become an economic powerhouse, driving marketing and consumer spending.

6. Community and Creativity

While modern Halloween has experienced a spike in commercialization, it remains to be a celebration that draws communities together. The ingenuity of costumes and decorations has no limitations, with individuals frequently striving to construct the most extravagant and innovative displays.

Modern Halloween has effectively combined the commercial components of the event with its more traditional and social features. It has developed into a celebration that appeals to persons of all ages, from youngsters delighted to don costumes and collect sweets to adults who find excitement in arranging extravagant parties or touring frightening places.

In the next chapters, we will go further into the global variants of Halloween, studying how different cultures have embraced and altered the festival, and evaluating the issues and critiques that have developed in the contemporary period. Despite its growth over decades, Halloween is a treasured and ever-evolving celebration of the unknown and the macabre.

Chapter 6
Global Variations

Halloween, a holiday with ancient Celtic and Roman roots, has developed through the years and extended far beyond its original homelands. It has evolved to the diverse cultures, customs, and beliefs of numerous locations across the world. The various variants of Halloween demonstrate the enthralling ways in which this holiday has been adopted and assimilated into many communities.

1. Halloween Around the World

A. Mexico - Día de los Muertos

In Mexico, Halloween is interwoven with Día de los Muertos, the Day of the Dead. Celebrated from October 31st to November 2nd, it's a time to commemorate dead loved ones. Families make ofrendas (altars) decked with marigolds, sugar skulls, and the favorite meals and drinks of the deceased. Calacas (skeletons) and calaveras (skulls) are common emblems, typically painted on faces or turned into masks. It's a combination of indigenous customs and Catholicism.

B. China - Teng Chieh

In China, Halloween is related with Teng Chieh, a celebration that remembers the deceased. Families honor dead relatives with offerings of food and presents, which are deposited on altars and at gravesites. Teng Chieh takes place on the 15th day of the seventh lunar month, generally corresponding to late August or early September.

C. Japan - Obon

Japan celebrates a similar event called as Obon, often around mid-August. It's a period when ancestor spirits are thought to return to the earthly realm. Families hang lamps to lead the spirits, visit cemeteries, and give offerings.

2. Diaspora Influence on Local Customs

Halloween has also been heavily impacted by expatriate cultures across the world. For example, in the United States, customs from diverse immigrant groups have contributed to the Halloween celebration.

Irish Influence: The habit of pumpkin carving may be traced back to the Irish immigrants, who brought the practice of carving turnips and potatoes in their homeland.

Mexican Influence: In locations with a substantial Mexican-American population, Día de los Muertos traditions have blended with Halloween, producing to celebrations that incorporate both cultural elements

Chinese Influence: In certain Chinese-American communities, Teng Chieh practices have affected the way Halloween is observed.

3. New Traditions in Other Cultures

As Halloween has grown internationally, new rituals have evolved in different regions.
United Kingdom: In the UK, Halloween parties and the practice of trick-or-treating have become increasingly prevalent in recent years, following the American model.
Philippines: In the Philippines, Pangangaluluwa is a ritual when children visit households and sing for the souls in purgatory, asking for prayers and donations in exchange.
Australia: Australians have inherited various Halloween customs, generally with a major focus on costumes and festivities, despite the holiday's little historical history in the nation.

4. Adaptation to Local Beliefs and Customs

In many countries, Halloween has been altered to match with local beliefs and customs. For example, in primarily Hindu India, Halloween celebrations may blend with the holiday of Diwali, the festival of lights. In largely Muslim nations, Halloween may not be commonly observed owing to cultural and theological differences.

The various variants of Halloween reflect its plasticity and capacity to adapt to the cultures and traditions of different locations. While the essential aspects of Halloween, such as costumes and the spirit of fun, remain consistent, the festival takes on a vast array of distinct and different forms across the world, reflecting the cultural fabric of mankind.

Chapter 7

Haunted Houses and Urban Legends

Halloween, with its atmosphere of mystery and the mysterious, has long been connected with haunted homes and urban tales. These spooky and exhilarating components of the event have become crucial to the current celebration of Halloween. In this section, we will study the obsession with haunted homes and the persistent power of urban tales.

1. The Birth of Haunted Attractions

The habit of making haunted houses for Halloween stretches back to the early 20th century. Initially, these attractions were generally set up in houses or improvised settings and were very modest in scale. They relied on basic methods, such concealed trapdoors, gloomy passages, and unsettling sound effects, to create a frightening environment.

As Halloween grew increasingly popular in the mid-20th century, professional haunted attractions began to develop. These were extravagant shows, involving sophisticated sets, dressed performers, and spectacular effects. Some of these attractions blossomed into enormous, well-known theme parks, dedicated completely to producing spine-tingling experiences.

2. Iconic Urban Legends

Halloween has a tight link with **urban legends**, typically propagated through storytelling and the media. These tales, often horrifying and strange, grab the imagination of people who hear them. Some popular Halloween-related urban legends include:

The Vanishing Hitchhiker: This tale describes the account of a mystery hitchhiker who disappears from a car during the trip, leaving behind only a trace of her presence.

The Babysitter and the Man Upstairs: In this popular urban legend, a babysitter receives scary phone calls from a stranger who confesses that he is inside the house with her.

The Hook-Handed Killer: This narrative focuses on a couple parked in an isolated spot when they hear about an escaped killer with a hook for a hand. As the narrative unfolds, they uncover a bloody hook on the car door handle.

3. Role of Media and Entertainment

Urban legends and haunted homes have been established in popular culture, owing in part to literature, movies, and television series. Horror films have played a crucial part in the propagation of urban legends and the representation of haunted houses. Titles like "Poltergeist," "The Amityville Horror," and "The Conjuring" have become famous in the horror genre.

Television productions like "Unsolved Mysteries" and "The X-Files" have further spurred interest in urban legends and the paranormal, contributing to their continuing popularity.

4. The Emergence of Commercial Haunted Attractions

Haunted attractions, typically situated in real-life settings, have achieved great appeal. These attractions range from haunted houses to haunted hayrides to haunted mazes. Commercial haunted attractions frequently combine sophisticated sets, skilled performers, and immersive narrative to produce dramatic, participatory experiences.

Haunted Theme Parks: Some theme parks, such as Universal Studios' Halloween Horror Nights, have become known for their haunted mazes and fear zones, bringing tourists from across the world.

Interactive Haunts: In recent years, interactive and intense haunts have attracted popularity. These experiences test the bounds of terror, requiring participants to sign agreements and often involve physical contact with performers.

5. The Lure of Fear

Haunted homes and urban tales continue to intrigue people, since they give a safe location to experience terror and the otherworldly. Many individuals are lured to the adrenaline rush and the excitement of being startled in a controlled situation. Haunted homes and urban tales allow us to confront our concerns and feel a sensation of danger without actual risk.

The obsession with haunted homes and urban stories adds a dimension of complexity to Halloween, making it a celebration not just for youngsters collecting treats but also for people seeking the adventure of the unknown. It encapsulates the spirit of Halloween and the persistent fascination of the spooky and the mysterious.

Chapter 8
The Evolution of Costumes

Costumes have always been an important element of Halloween, converting it into a time for creativity, self-expression, and social celebration. Halloween costumes have evolved throughout time to reflect evolving cultural, social, and technological influences.

1. Early Costumes: Disguising and Dispelling Spirits

The custom of dressing up for Halloween dates back to the ancient Celtic celebration of Samhain. To fend off evil spirits, the Celts would disguise themselves with animal skins and heads. Wearing costumes as a measure of defense or disguise has evolved into an important aspect of Halloween.

2. The Victorian Era: The Origins of Themed Parties

Halloween took on a more social and romantic tone throughout the Victorian era, and costume parties were fashionable. These events included elaborate, historically-inspired costumes. The emphasis was on creativity and self-expression, with guests taking on the roles of legendary figures and literary heroes.

3. Commercial Costumes and Popular Icons in the Early Twentieth Century

Commercial costumes first appeared in the early twentieth century. People were able to engage in Halloween events more easily because to these pre-packaged clothes. Traditional Halloween figures such as witches, ghosts, and pumpkins were popular options.

Costumes influenced by popular culture, such as cinema stars, comic book characters, and historical people, were fashionable in the 1920s and 1930s. The availability of new materials made it possible to create more complex and elaborate costume designs.

4. Television's Influence in the 1950s and 1960s

The postwar period saw the birth of a new cultural phenomenon: television. As TV series became more popular, so did costumes based on TV characters. Children, in particular, began dressing up like characters from shows such as "Superman," "The Lone Ranger," and "The Addams Family."

5. The Rise of Licensed Characters in the 1970s and 1980s

The 1970s and 1980s saw the rise of licensed character outfits. Iconic movie, cartoon, and comic book characters became widely available, turning Halloween into a marketing opportunity for entertainment corporations. During this time period, there was a boom in demand for costumes based on popular figures such as Darth Vader, Mickey Mouse, and Superman.

6. Pop Culture and DIY from the 1990s to the Present

The late twentieth and early twenty-first centuries saw a wide diversity of clothing styles. Characters from movies, TV shows, and video games have dominated the costume scene for decades.

DIY costumes have seen an increase in popularity in recent years. Many people like making their own clothes, which are often inspired by their favorite characters or innovative thoughts. Individuals can now present their homemade costumes more easily thanks to online guides and social media, and the DIY craze has become an essential part of modern Halloween.

7. Cultural Sensitivity and Inclusivity

There is a rising understanding of the necessity of inclusive and culturally sensitive clothing in recent years. Cultural appropriation as well as rude outfits have been criticized. Many individuals now try to pick costumes that respect other people's cultural history and traditions.

Costumes for Halloween have progressed from simple disguises to intricate demonstrations of creativity and individuality. They have reflected evolving cultural, technological, and entertainment influences. In essence, Halloween has evolved into an annual celebration of imagination and uniqueness, in which individuals can change themselves into anything they choose, if only for one wonderful evening.

Chapter 9

Jack-o'-Lanterns

Jack-o'-lanterns are one of Halloween's most recognizable and enduring emblems. These carved pumpkins, lit by a candle or an LED light, have become an essential aspect of the holiday's visual identity. The practice of carving jack-o'-lanterns is deep in history and legend, and it remains a popular Halloween ritual.

1. Celtic Origins: The Will-o'-the-Wisp

Jack-o'-lanterns have their origins in Celtic tradition and the ancient celebration of Samhain. The Celts thought that at Samhain, the line between the living and the dead became blurred, allowing ghosts to roam freely. They would light bonfires and set turnip lanterns near their dwellings to fend off these wandering souls and malicious spirits.

They told stories of a strange phenomena known as the "will-o'-the-wisp" or "ignis fatuus." This was a weird light that flickered over swamps and marshes, and it was commonly connected with evil or mischievous spirits. The Celts considered these lights to be guiding spirits and attempted to imitate them by making their own lanterns.

2. Transformation into Pumpkin Lanterns

Irish immigrants brought the tradition of carving jack-o'-lanterns to North America in the nineteenth century. They realized that pumpkins, which were natural to the region, were better suited for carving than turnips in their new home. Turnips were substituted as the canvas for these frightening lanterns by enormous, spherical, easily hollowed-out pumpkins.

3. The Legend of Stingy Jack

The term "jack-o'-lantern" comes from the Irish folktale "Stingy Jack." Stingy Jack was a crafty guy who played pranks on the devil, according to folklore. He was neither welcomed into paradise nor admitted into hell when he died. Instead, he was sentenced to travel the world with nothing but a smoldering coal inside a turnip to guide him. To fend off Stingy Jack and other roaming ghosts, people began to create their own lanterns.

4. Modern Jack-o-Lanterns

Jack-o'-lanterns are now an integral feature of Halloween festivities. The process of making these holiday lanterns has become a favorite pastime for families and friends. Typically, the steps are as follows:

Pumpkin Selection: The first step is to select the ideal pumpkin. Its size, form, and condition can all have an impact on the design options.

Carving: The creative process begins once the top is taken off and the interior is hollowed out. Traditional designs frequently incorporate eerie faces, while modern jack-o'-lanterns can have detailed patterns, scenery, or even homage to popular personalities.

illumination: A candle or an LED light is inserted within the carved pumpkin to provide a pleasant, flickering glow.

5. Contemporary Art

While traditional jack-o'-lantern designs are still popular, current carvers have elevated the art form to new heights. Pumpkin artisans use many pumpkins to construct elaborate, three-dimensional sculptures, which are displayed at pumpkin festivals across the world.

6. The Symbolism of Light

Jack-o'-lanterns function as both festive decorations and protective symbols. Their glow is said to fend off evil spirits and guide helpful spirits. They are also utilized as beacons for trick-or-treaters, illuminating the route to homes on Halloween night.

Finally, the simple jack-o'-lantern has a long and illustrious history that combines Celtic tradition, Irish legend, and American inventiveness. In the spirit of Halloween, it is a treasured custom that draws families and communities together, combining the past with the present.

Chapter 10
Spooky Treats

Halloween isn't just about costumes and decorations; it's also a chance to indulge on a variety of tasty and cleverly themed delicacies. From candy and pastries to ghoulish beverages, the world of scary goodies is a wonderful and vital element of Halloween celebrations. In this part, we'll examine the broad array of frightening sweets that make Halloween a gastronomic experience.

1. Trick-or-Treat Candy

Trick-or-treating is at the core of Halloween, and it's all about the candy. Children and adults alike excitedly await filling their bags with a broad assortment of chocolates, from classics to seasonal favorites:

Candy Corn: These classic tri-colored sweets are fashioned like corn kernels and are synonymous with Halloween.

Chocolate Bars: Miniature chocolate bars, frequently sporting Halloween-themed wrappers, are a cherished delicacy.

Gummies and Jellies: Gummy worms, spiders, and bats are popular choices, as are jelly-filled candies in varied flavors.

Lollipops: Halloween-themed lollipops commonly feature forms like skulls, pumpkins, or ghosts.

2. Baked Goods

Halloween is the best time for creative baking. From frightening cookies to luscious desserts, the choices are endless:

Halloween Cookies: These might take the style of witches' hats, mummies, or black cats, covered with colored icing.

Pumpkin Pie: A popular dish that's a mainstay during the fall, commonly savored on Thanksgiving as well.

Cupcakes: Halloween cupcakes come in all sorts of styles and tastes, topped with seasonal decorations.

Caramel Apples: Apples covered in caramel and garnished with numerous toppings, from nuts to candies, make for a lovely delicacy.

3. Creepy Confections

Halloween gives sufficient inspiration for producing creative and spooky confections:

Monster Eyeballs: Litchi fruit or stuffed olives create fantastic scary "eyeballs" when set in a bed of cream cheese and decorated with ketchup.

Witch's Brew Punch: Green or purple punch mixed with flavored sodas, sherbet, and gummy monsters is a fun and terrifying drink for parties.

Spider Web Cakes: A cake embellished with a spider web pattern using icing or chocolate ganache provides a hauntingly gorgeous centerpiece.

4. Themed Beverages

In addition to chocolates and baked items, Halloween-themed beverages are a requirement for parties and gatherings:

Hot Cider: Warm apple cider spiked with cinnamon and served with a cinnamon stick is a comfortable and classic fall beverage.

Witches' Brew: This dark and spooky cocktail can be created with grape juice, blackberries, and soda, topped with floating "eyeballs" formed from lychee fruit or grapes.

Blood Orange Punch: Mixing blood orange juice with sparkling water and a dash of grenadine produces a visually spectacular and delectable cocktail.

5. International Spooky Treats

Halloween-inspired delicacies differ across the world. In Mexico, sugar skulls are prepared as part of Día de los Muertos celebrations. In Ireland and the UK, barmbrack, a fruitcake containing hidden secrets, is popular. In Japan, Halloween-themed Pocky sticks are a beloved snack.

6. The Joy of Spooky Treats

Halloween sweets aren't just about gratifying a sweet appetite; they reflect the spirit of the season and give a feeling of creativity and enjoyment. Whether you're savoring classic candy, baking frightening cookies with loved ones, or sipping a witch's brew at a Halloween party, these delights enhance the festive mood and contribute to the magic of the season.

Spooky snacks are a reminder that Halloween is a time when the imagination takes center stage, both in the creation of the delicacies and in the delight of consuming them. They enable us to play with our food and appreciate the playful part of the celebration.

Chapter 11

Traditions for the Paranormal

Halloween's origins are strongly steeped in the supernatural and the notion that, around this time of year, the line between the living and the dead is at its thinnest. Throughout history, numerous customs have evolved that are dedicated to studying the paranormal and the scary, bringing an added element of intrigue to the event.

1. Séances and Spirit Communication

Séances have a long history, and they are generally connected with Halloween and the desire to speak with the departed. In a séance, people assemble in a dimly lit room, clasp hands, and attempt to establish contact with spirits. A medium or spiritualist typically conducts the events. The participants may ask questions or seek signals from the other side, with replies typically appearing through raps, knocks, or the movement of items.

2. Divination and Fortune-Telling

Halloween has a strong relationship with fortune-telling and divination. People have participated in numerous strategies to foresee their future, particularly in the context of romance and relationships. Some prominent divination rituals include:

Apple Bobbing: Participants attempt to snag an apple with their teeth while it floats in a tank of water, with each fruit equating to a different fate.

Mirror-staring: This ritual includes staring into a mirror on Halloween night to obtain a glimpse of one's future spouse.

Tarot Cards: Many persons turn to tarot card readings on Halloween to obtain insights into their destiny.

Ouija Boards: Ouija boards are typically taken out on Halloween to speak with spirits or get messages from the other side.

3. Visiting Cemeteries and Haunted Locations

with those with a special curiosity with the paranormal, Halloween is a perfect time to visit cemeteries and other haunted locales. These trips might feature guided tours, during which guests may learn about the history and mythology surrounding these places, as well as the purported hauntings that have occurred there.

4. Telling Ghost Stories

The habit of exchanging ghost stories is a typical Halloween ritual. Whether over a campfire or by candlelight, people narrate tales of apparitions, haunted houses, and inexplicable events. Some ghost stories are passed down through generations, while others are produced anew each year.

5. Día de los Muertos

Día de los Muertos, or Day of the Dead, is a Mexican holiday that commonly corresponds with Halloween. It is a time to commemorate and celebrate deceased loved ones by building ofrendas (altars) covered with offerings like marigolds, sugar skulls, and the favorite meals and drinks of the departed. Families may visit cemeteries to clean and decorate graves.

6. The Great Pumpkin Tradition

In more recent years, the "Great Pumpkin" tradition, popularized by Charles M. Schulz's Peanuts comic strips and the animated TV special, "It's the Great Pumpkin, Charlie Brown," has become a celebrated aspect of Halloween. In this custom, youngsters think that the "Great Pumpkin" will visit pumpkin patches and offer presents to sincere, well-behaved children on Halloween night.

7. Wiccan and Pagan Celebrations

For many current Wiccans and Neopagans, Halloween, or Samhain, is a sacred holiday. They consider it as a time to commemorate their ancestors, perform rituals, and celebrate the cycle of life and death. Bonfires and the construction of altars for the departed are popular customs during these ceremonies.

8. Midnight Cemetery Visits

Some persons indulge in the ritual of visiting a graveyard at midnight on Halloween night. It is claimed that the line between the realms of the living and the dead is the thinnest at this time, making it easier to interact with ghosts or observe paranormal activities.

Halloween's relationship to the paranormal is a source of interest and magic for many. The traditions linked with séances, divination, cemetery visits, and ghost stories give a chance to explore the unknown and connect with the mysteries of life and death. Whether taken literally or in the spirit of fun, these customs give dimension to the Halloween experience and offer a view into the world of the unexplained.

Chapter 12
Halloween in Pop Culture

Halloween has had a huge influence on pop culture, becoming a prominent and adored component of the entertainment business. This section discusses how Halloween has left an everlasting influence on numerous kinds of pop culture, from cinema and television to music, literature, and more.

1. Halloween in Film

Horror Films: Halloween has been the setting for innumerable horror films. Classics like "Halloween" (1978) and "Nightmare on Elm Street" (1984) have become legendary, while modern movies continue to delight and frighten audiences.

Family-Friendly Films: For a younger audience, Halloween-themed movies like "Hocus Pocus" (1993) and "The Nightmare Before Christmas" (1993) have become yearly rituals.

Comedy-Horror: Films like "Beetlejuice" (1988) and "The Addams Family" (1991) merge humor with the macabre, presenting a lighter perspective on Halloween.

Paranormal and Supernatural Themes: Movies like "Ghostbusters" (1984) and "The Sixth Sense" (1999) explore into paranormal and supernatural phenomena, frequently with a feeling of mystery and intrigue.

2. Halloween on Television

Halloween Specials: TV programs regularly air Halloween-themed episodes, becoming popular yearly traditions. Classics include "It's the Great Pumpkin, Charlie Brown" and "The Simpsons' Treehouse of Horror" episodes.

Reality and Competition Shows: Television shows have also gotten in on the Halloween fun, with series like "Halloween Wars" showing inventive pumpkin carving and cake decorating competitions.

Live Events: Halloween specials, like "The Rocky Horror Picture Show," have been recreated as live events, reaching new generations of fans.

3. Music and Halloween Soundtracks:

Halloween soundtracks: comprising creepy music and terrifying sound effects, establish the tone for Halloween events and haunted attractions.

Halloween-Themed Songs: Songs like "Thriller" by Michael Jackson, "Monster Mash" by Bobby Pickett, and "This Is Halloween" from "The Nightmare Before Christmas" are staples of Halloween playlists.

Musical Events: Some musicians enjoy Halloween with dramatic live events, such as Alice Cooper's yearly Halloween concert.

4. Literature and Halloween

Halloween-Themed Books: Various authors have created Halloween-themed books for various ages. Classics like "Scary Stories to Tell in the Dark" by Alvin Schwartz have been read by generations of children.

Horror books: Horror books typically contain Halloween themes, with authors like Stephen King giving spine-tingling readings suitable for the season.

Witchcraft and Magic: Books about witchcraft and magic have enjoyed a comeback in popularity, in part owing to Halloween's focus on the mysterious and otherworldly.

5. Halloween in Fashion

Costumes: Halloween costumes are not restricted to a single night. Costume fashion trends often impact the business throughout the year, with "cosplay" becoming a popular activity year-round.

Spooky Fashion Trends: Fashion designers draw inspiration from Halloween, designing clothing lines with eerie patterns like skulls, cobwebs, and bats.

6. Halloween on Social Media

#Halloween: The introduction of social media has given rise to hashtag fads, such as #Halloween, when people post costume ideas, macabre foods, and DIY décor.

Viral Challenges: Challenges like the "Pumpkin Spice Challenge" and the "Pumpkin Carving Challenge" have garnered popularity on sites like YouTube and TikTok.

7. Halloween-Themed Products

Food and Beverages: Many firms produce limited-edition Halloween-themed items, from pumpkin spice lattes to cereals with Halloween shapes and flavors.

Products: Retailers load their shelves with Halloween-themed products, including clothes, accessories, home décor, and collectibles.

Halloween has invaded practically every facet of pop culture, becoming a beloved and lively festival that crosses generational and cultural borders. Its effect on movies, television, music, literature, fashion, and more continues to expand, making Halloween not simply a holiday but a cultural phenomenon that affects entertainment and creativity throughout the year.

Chapter 13

Commercialization of Halloween

Halloween, originally a simple and humble holiday with deep-rooted traditions, has seen a tremendous alteration during the past century. It has developed from a day of modest festivity to a highly marketed affair. In this part, we'll study the commercialization of Halloween and how it has affected the present celebration of this cherished holiday.

1. Historical Context

The commercialization of Halloween began in earnest in the early 20th century, particularly in the United States. This transition was driven by a convergence of causes, including urbanization, industrialization, and the expansion of the consumer culture. Key aspects contributing to this trend include:

Department Stores: The emergence of huge department shops gave a platform for promoting Halloween-themed items. Stores began to dedicate whole areas to Halloween merchandise, from costumes to decorations.

Greeting Card Industry: The greeting card Industry played a key part in Halloween's commercialization, creating Halloween-themed cards and decorations.

2. The Rise of Halloween as a Retail Holiday

Halloween has developed into a multibillion-dollar industry. The commercialization of Halloween encompasses three main sectors:

Costumes: Halloween costumes have grown very intricate and specialized, with an ever-expanding number of alternatives, including licensed characters from famous movies and TV series.

Decorations: Inflatable monsters, animatronic witches, and sophisticated yard displays have become the norm for Halloween décor.

Candies: The demand for Halloween candies has expanded dramatically, with candy producers designing distinctive, Halloween-themed packaging.

Party Supplies: From dinnerware to party favors, a broad assortment of Halloween-themed Supplies are easily accessible.

Haunted Attractions: The industry of haunted homes and haunted mazes has risen considerably, delivering immersive and often intense experiences.

3. Globalization of Halloween Commercialization

The commercialization of Halloween is not restricted to the United States. Halloween has become a global phenomenon, with various nations embracing and modifying the economic components of the festival. For example:

Japan: Japan has embraced Halloween with related items, costumes, and decorations, even though it wasn't historically observed in the nation.

Australia: Halloween has gained popularity, with Australians buying costumes, decorations, and partaking in trick-or-treating.

4. Controversies and Criticisms

While the commercialization of Halloween has given economic benefits to different businesses, it has also caused debates and criticisms:

Cultural Appropriation: Some costumes and decorations have been condemned for promoting stereotypes and cultural appropriation.

Environmental problems: The creation and disposal of throwaway Halloween decorations add to environmental problems.

Commercialization: Critics believe that the concentration on commercialization takes away from the holiday's original ethos, promoting materialism over tradition.

5. Balance Between Commercial and Traditional Aspects

Despite its commercialization, Halloween remains a holiday that retains significant importance for many. People typically seek to create a balance between the commercial and traditional parts of the holiday. For some, Halloween signifies a time for creativity, self-expression, and the rekindling of traditions. Others view it as an occasion to celebrate with friends and family, whether through house decorations, DIY costumes, or a frightening movie night.

The commercialization of Halloween has changed the celebration into a complicated combination of tradition and materialism. While the commercial components of Halloween are evident, the festival continues to give a chance for communities and families to get together, show their creativity, and explore the spooky and the unexplained. As Halloween changes in the modern world, it remains a popular and ever-adapting celebration of the alluring and the spooky.

Chapter 14
The Future of Halloween

Halloween, with its rich history and ever-evolving traditions, is a holiday that continues to attract people throughout the world. As we look to the future, we may foresee some important trends and innovations that will affect the way Halloween is celebrated in the years to come.

1. Technology and Virtual Celebrations

Technology is set to play an increasingly major role in the future of Halloween. This may include:

Virtual Parties: As demonstrated during the COVID-19 epidemic, virtual Halloween parties and activities may give a safe and easy way to spend the holiday with friends and family from anywhere in the globe.

Augmented Reality (AR) and Virtual Reality (VR): AR and VR experiences might increase the way people interact with Halloween-themed material and games, providing immersive and engaging festivities.

2. Sustainability & Eco-Friendly Halloween

Environmental awareness and sustainability are emerging issues, and these ideas are likely to impact the future of Halloween in various ways:

Eco-Friendly Decorations: The usage of biodegradable or reusable decorations, as well as DIY crafts created from recyclable materials, will become increasingly prevalent.

Sustainable Costumes: People may pick sustainable and ethical costume alternatives, and upcycling old garments to make costumes will be emphasized.

Local and Seasonal Focus: Emphasis on choosing locally produced and seasonal materials for Halloween snacks and decorations will lessen the carbon impact.

3. Inclusivity and Cultural Sensitivity

The relevance of cultural sensitivity and tolerance is projected to expand. Halloween will become more courteous and tolerant of other cultures and traditions:

Education: Schools and communities may place a greater focus on teaching people about the cultural importance of Halloween and Día de los Muertos and other comparable festivals.

Appropriateness in Costumes: Guidelines for suitable costumes may become more commonly understood and followed, minimizing instances of cultural appropriation.

4. Blending of Traditions

Halloween, as it develops internationally, will continue to merge with various customs and holidays:

Día de los Muertos: The merger of Halloween and Día de los Muertos traditions will certainly become more evident, resulting to a unique and rich cultural interaction.

Harvest Celebrations: In places where Halloween coincides with harvest celebrations, we should expect a continual mingling of the two, integrating agricultural traditions with the spookiness of Halloween.

5. Creative and Inclusive Costumes

Halloween costumes will continue to reflect shifting cultural attitudes:

Inclusive Costumes: Expect to see a broader selection of inclusive costumes reflecting all genders, abilities, and cultures.

DIY & Homemade Costumes: The DIY costume trend is expected to expand as individuals seek inventive and individualized ways to celebrate Halloween.

6. Community Engagement

The idea of community and connection will remain at the core of Halloween:

Local activities: Communities will offer more local activities, such as Halloween parades, costume contests, and neighborhood decoration contests.

Philanthropic Activities: Incorporating philanthropic activities, such as food drives and fundraising events, into Halloween celebrations will grow increasingly prevalent.

7. Adaptation to Current Events

Halloween has always altered to reflect the present zeitgeist, and it will continue to do so:

Masks and Health Safety: Given the health concerns in the post-COVID period, face masks may become a popular costume piece.

Political and Social Themes: Halloween costumes may increasingly reflect contemporary political and social events, as demonstrated with recent trends in political satire and activism.

In the future, Halloween will remain a dynamic and adaptive festival, taking on new shapes and incorporating other cultural influences. Its underlying spirit of creativity, community, and celebration of the supernatural will continue to appeal with people of all ages, making it a festival that endures and evolves for decades to come.

Thank you for joining me on this journey through the history and traditions of Halloween. I hope you've enjoyed exploring the fascinating world of this beloved holiday as much as I've enjoyed sharing it with you. If you found this book informative and engaging, please consider sharing it with friends, family, and fellow Halloween enthusiasts. Your support in spreading the word is invaluable.

If you'd like to help this book reach even more readers, leaving a review on the platform where you purchased it would be greatly appreciated. Reviews provide valuable feedback and help others discover this work.

For those who want to explore Halloween further or gift this book to others who share the same passion, consider purchasing additional copies. You can find more information on where to purchase more copies and other works by the author on Amazon.

Thank you once again for your time and interest in the world of Halloween. Wishing you a spooktacular and festive Halloween season!"